Can't I have a moment to myself

S. Page

Published by S. Page, 2024.

CAN'T I HAVE A MOMENT TO MYSELF

First edition. December 27, 2024.

ISBN: 979-8230573906

Written by S. Page.

Prologue

The Journey Begins With You

I used to think that self-love was a luxury. Something you had to work hard for, something that came with a perfectly curated life—one full of social media-worthy moments, flawless skin, and career success. I thought self-love was about perfecting yourself, about being a glowing, confident version of you at all times. Spoiler alert: I was wrong.

This book isn't about that kind of perfection. This is a story about learning to love yourself—not when you have it all figured out, but right in the middle of the chaos, the mess, and the moments of self-doubt. It's about figuring out who you are, even when you feel lost, and learning how to treat yourself with kindness, humor, and grace along the way.

Self-love isn't something that happens overnight. It's a messy, awkward, beautiful, and often frustrating journey. It's like trying to figure out how to dance when you've never had a lesson in your life. You'll stumble, you'll laugh, and you'll wonder if it's worth it. But trust me, it is.

I know what it's like to feel unworthy, to put everyone else's needs before your own, to get lost in the expectations of others. I've been there. And that's why I want to share this with you—because I'm here to tell you that you are enough. Right now. Exactly as you are. And this book? This book is a reminder of that truth.

This isn't a "how-to" guide filled with unrealistic tips or tricks. It's a journey—a series of stories, reflections, and lessons that will hopefully make you laugh, cringe, and maybe even cry a little (in a good way). But most importantly, it's a book that encourages you to start where you are, to embrace your imperfections, and to move forward with compassion for yourself.

So, if you've ever felt like you're not good enough, not worthy enough, or not something enough, this is for you. If you've ever looked in the mirror and wondered how to love the person staring back at you, this is for you. Because self-love isn't about being perfect—it's about accepting yourself just as you are.

Welcome to the journey. Let's begin.

Introduction

I wrote this book to inspire the next person to look past that layer of not trusting one's self worth. Always remember "Love" has no bounds.

Chapter 1: You're Not Broken, You're Just Weird (Like Everyone Else)

Let me tell you a story about the time I thought I was irreparably broken. It was a Tuesday, and I couldn't decide what to wear to a Zoom meeting. Yes, a Zoom meeting. No one was going to see anything below my shoulders, but I spent 30 minutes debating whether my pajama bottoms clashed with my cat sweatshirt. I ended up crying on the floor, clutching a bag of Doritos, wondering why I couldn't get my life together.

And then it hit me: everyone's life is just a series of weird, chaotic, pajama-clad moments. My meltdown didn't mean I was broken—it just meant I was human (and maybe needed less caffeine).

—-

The Truth About Being "Broken"

You're not broken. You're just unique. Think of it this way: every time you feel like a mess, remember that the Mona Lisa is basically a mess of tiny brushstrokes, and people still line up to stare at her mysterious smirk.

Society loves to tell us we're not good enough. We don't wake up at 5 AM to journal? Lazy. We eat a whole pizza in one sitting? Unhealthy. We spend three hours watching hamster obstacle courses on YouTube? Irrelevant. But who gets to decide what's "normal"? Because let's face it, normal is boring, and pizza is delicious.

—-

The Beauty of Weirdness

You know that thing you do when you try to laugh quietly but it comes out like a seal barking? That's gold. Or how you sometimes dance in the kitchen with a spatula as your microphone? Iconic. Those little quirks make you you.

In fact, the world needs your weirdness. Imagine if everyone were perfectly put-together all the time. No bad hair days. No ugly crying. No randomly quoting Shrek during serious conversations. We'd all be Stepford robots, and let's be honest, no one wants that.

—-

Self-Love Exercise: The Weirdness Inventory

Take five minutes and list the top three things that make you weird.

Do you collect tiny plastic dinosaurs and make them have dramatic soap opera arguments?

Do you eat peanut butter straight out of the jar at midnight while humming the theme song from The Office?

Do you always say "bless you" to your dog when they sneeze?

Write them down and celebrate them. These quirks are what make you unforgettable.

—-

Punchline Takeaway

You don't need to be fixed because you were never broken. You're a limited edition, one-of-a-kind masterpiece. Like a Picasso painting, but with better eyebrows.

Chapter 2: Your Inner Critic is a Drama Queen

Opening Anecdote: The Inner Critic Goes Overboard

Picture this: you're about to post a selfie. It's a good hair day, the lighting is chef's kiss, and you even nailed that effortless "I just woke up like this" look. You're ready to hit post when a little voice pops up in your head:

"Your nose looks weird. Why are your eyebrows uneven? Are you sure people want to see this?"

And just like that, your inner critic transforms a perfectly good moment into an emotional courtroom drama, with you as both the defendant and the harshest judge.

The truth is, your inner critic is less of a wise advisor and more like a dramatic aunt who turns every family gathering into a soap opera. So why are we listening to her?

—-

Meet Your Inner Critic: The Overdramatic Villain

Let's give your inner critic a personality because nothing takes the power out of a bully like making them ridiculous. Imagine this:

She's wearing a sparkly cape and stomping around, yelling, "You're a failure!" every time you burn toast.

She sits in the backseat of your life, eating chips loudly while making snarky comments about your driving skills (literally and metaphorically).

The inner critic thrives on exaggeration. If you forget one thing on your to-do list, she'll whisper, "Well, I guess you're a total disaster now!" It's time to put her in her place.

—-

Why Your Inner Critic Exists (And Why She's Kind of Dumb)

The inner critic isn't entirely evil. She's just your brain's way of trying to protect you from failure, rejection, or embarrassment. Back in caveman days, this was helpful—"Don't fight that tiger; you're not fast enough!" But now? Not so much.

In modern life, she's warning you about non-life-threatening things, like wearing the wrong shoes to a party. And the worst part? She's often wrong. When was the last time someone actually cared about your shoes?

—-

Exercise: Name Your Inner Critic

To take her less seriously, give her a silly name. Mine is "Gertrude the Grump." Here's why this works:

When Gertrude starts yammering about how I'm "not good enough," I can roll my eyes and say, "Thanks for the input, Gert, but I've got this."

Naming her reminds me that she's separate from me.

Take a moment and name your inner critic. Is she "Debbie Downer"? "Negative Nancy"? "Chad the Complainer"? Pick something that makes you laugh, because laughter is kryptonite to negativity.

—-

Inner Critic vs. Inner Cheerleader

Here's the deal: for every snarky comment your inner critic makes, your inner cheerleader deserves equal air time. If your critic says, "You'll never finish this project," your cheerleader can shout back, "But look how much you've already done!"

Imagine them having a debate:

Critic: "You messed up that presentation!"

Cheerleader: "Yeah, but you nailed the Q&A session afterward."

Practice giving your inner cheerleader a voice. If she's shy, think of a supportive friend and channel them. Or better yet, pretend Beyoncé is hyping you up.

—-

Funny Ways to Shut Your Inner Critic Down

1. The Dramatic Clapback: When your critic says, "You're terrible at this," respond, "Thanks for the TED Talk, but I didn't ask."

2. The Mute Button: Visualize holding a remote control and pressing "mute" whenever the critic starts talking. Bonus points if you imagine them looking offended.

3. The Dance-Off: Interrupt negative thoughts with a ridiculous dance break. Nothing deflates criticism like bad moonwalking.

—-

Quick Reframe: Is This Fact or Fiction?

Whenever your critic pipes up, ask yourself:

1. Is this actually true? ("Everyone will hate me if I speak up." Really? Everyone?)

2. What's the worst that could happen? (So what if you trip on stage? Instant comedy.)

3. What would I say to a friend in this situation? Spoiler: You'd be way nicer to them than you are to yourself.

—-

Pop Culture Heroes Who Didn't Listen to Their Critics

Taylor Swift: People told her she couldn't sing. She made a career out of proving them wrong.

Steve Jobs: Got fired from his own company. Came back and changed the world.

The Grinch: Okay, maybe not a role model, but he did overcome self-doubt and save Christmas.

—-

Exercise: Turn Your Critic Into Comedy

The next time your inner critic starts ranting, write down what she says. Then exaggerate it until it's ridiculous. Example:

Critic: "You'll never succeed at this project."

Exaggerated version: "You'll fail so hard that your ancestors will feel embarrassed."

New response: "Wow, that's dramatic. Did you write this for a Netflix series?"

Laughing at your critic is the fastest way to take away her power.

—-

The Big Takeaway

Your inner critic isn't the boss of you. She's just a noisy backseat driver who thinks she knows the directions better than Google Maps. The next time she pipes up, thank her for her opinion, then turn up your mental playlist of empowering jams and keep driving.

Because here's the truth: You are so much more than your doubts. You're the one behind the wheel, and your destination? Unstoppable greatness.

—-

Should we add another interactive exercise or expand further into specific scenarios where people often face inner criticism (like at work, in relationships, etc.)? Let me know!

Chapter 2: Your Inner Critic is a Drama Queen

The Inner Critic Goes Overboard

Picture this: you're about to post a selfie. It's a good hair day, the lighting is chef's kiss, and you even nailed that effortless "I just woke up like this" look. You're ready to hit post when a little voice pops up in your head:

"Your nose looks weird. Why are your eyebrows uneven? Are you sure people want to see this?"

And just like that, your inner critic transforms a perfectly good moment into an emotional courtroom drama, with you as both the defendant and the harshest judge.

The truth is, your inner critic is less of a wise advisor and more like a dramatic aunt who turns every family gathering into a soap opera. So why are we listening to her?

—-

Meet Your Inner Critic: The Overdramatic Villain

Let's give your inner critic a personality because nothing takes the power out of a bully like making them ridiculous. Imagine this:

She's wearing a sparkly cape and stomping around, yelling, "You're a failure!" every time you burn toast.

She sits in the backseat of your life, eating chips loudly while making snarky comments about your driving skills (literally and metaphorically).

The inner critic thrives on exaggeration. If you forget one thing on your to-do list, she'll whisper, "Well, I guess you're a total disaster now!" It's time to put her in her place.

—-

Why Your Inner Critic Exists (And Why She's Kind of Dumb)

The inner critic isn't entirely evil. She's just your brain's way of trying to protect you from failure, rejection, or embarrassment. Back in caveman days, this was helpful—"Don't fight that tiger; you're not fast enough!" But now? Not so much.

In modern life, she's warning you about non-life-threatening things, like wearing the wrong shoes to a party. And the worst part? She's often wrong. When was the last time someone actually cared about your shoes?

—-

Exercise: Name Your Inner Critic

To take her less seriously, give her a silly name. Mine is "Gertrude the Grump." Here's why this works:

When Gertrude starts yammering about how I'm "not good enough," I can roll my eyes and say, "Thanks for the input, Gert, but I've got this."

Naming her reminds me that she's separate from me.

Take a moment and name your inner critic. Is she "Debbie Downer"? "Negative Nancy"? "Chad the Complainer"? Pick something that makes you laugh, because laughter is kryptonite to negativity.

—-

Inner Critic vs. Inner Cheerleader

Here's the deal: for every snarky comment your inner critic makes, your inner cheerleader deserves equal air time. If your critic says, "You'll never finish this project," your cheerleader can shout back, "But look how much you've already done!"

Imagine them having a debate:

Critic: "You messed up that presentation!"

Cheerleader: "Yeah, but you nailed the Q&A session afterward."

Practice giving your inner cheerleader a voice. If she's shy, think of a supportive friend and channel them. Or better yet, pretend Beyoncé is hyping you up.

—-

Funny Ways to Shut Your Inner Critic Down

1. The Dramatic Clapback: When your critic says, "You're terrible at this," respond, "Thanks for the TED Talk, but I didn't ask."

2. The Mute Button: Visualize holding a remote control and pressing "mute" whenever the critic starts talking. Bonus points if you imagine them looking offended.

3. The Dance-Off: Interrupt negative thoughts with a ridiculous dance break. Nothing deflates criticism like bad moonwalking.

—-

Quick Reframe: Is This Fact or Fiction?

Whenever your critic pipes up, ask yourself:

1. Is this actually true? ("Everyone will hate me if I speak up." Really? Everyone?)

2. What's the worst that could happen? (So what if you trip on stage? Instant comedy.)

3. What would I say to a friend in this situation? Spoiler: You'd be way nicer to them than you are to yourself.

—-

Pop Culture Heroes Who Didn't Listen to Their Critics

Taylor Swift: People told her she couldn't sing. She made a career out of proving them wrong.

Steve Jobs: Got fired from his own company. Came back and changed the world.

The Grinch: Okay, maybe not a role model, but he did overcome self-doubt and save Christmas.

—-

Exercise: Turn Your Critic Into Comedy

The next time your inner critic starts ranting, write down what she says. Then exaggerate it until it's ridiculous. Example:

Critic: "You'll never succeed at this project."

Exaggerated version: "You'll fail so hard that your ancestors will feel embarrassed."

New response: "Wow, that's dramatic. Did you write this for a Netflix series?"

Laughing at your critic is the fastest way to take away her power.

—-

The Big Takeaway

Your inner critic isn't the boss of you. She's just a noisy backseat driver who thinks she knows the directions better than Google Maps. The next time she pipes up, thank her for her opinion, then turn up your mental playlist of empowering jams and keep driving.

Because here's the truth: You are so much more than your doubts. You're the one behind the wheel, and your destination? Unstoppable greatness.

—-

Chapter 3: Self-Care is Not Selfish (But It Can Be Hilarious)

The Bubble Bath Debacle

It was a dark and stormy night. Okay, it was just a Tuesday, but it felt dramatic because I was on the brink of a meltdown. My solution? Self-care. I lit candles, poured some bubbles into the tub, and confidently stepped in—only to discover the water was freezing cold because I forgot to check the temperature.

So there I was, shivering and questioning every decision that led me to this moment. Was this self-care? Or just an elaborate prank I'd played on myself?

Here's the thing about self-care: It's not always pretty. Sometimes it's messy, awkward, or downright funny. But it's absolutely necessary.

—-

Self-Care is Not a Luxury, It's a Survival Strategy

Think of self-care like charging your phone. You wouldn't let your phone die mid-scroll on TikTok, so why let yourself run on 1%? And no, coffee doesn't count as a full charge—it's more like putting your phone on airplane mode for five minutes.

The truth is, taking care of yourself isn't selfish—it's the only way to show up for your life without turning into a cranky, sleep-deprived goblin.

—-

Part 1: What Self-Care Really Looks Like (Hint: It's Not All Spa Days)

The Myth of Instagram-Worthy Self-Care

We've all seen those posts: perfectly arranged avocado toast, pristine yoga poses, and someone lounging in a fluffy robe that costs more than your rent. While that's great for them, let's be real:

Your Reality: Eating cereal straight out of the box while binge-watching The Office.

Their Instagram Post: "Just did a 10-step skincare routine!"

Your Reality: Forgetting to moisturize and calling it "natural beauty."

Self-care doesn't have to be picture-perfect. Sometimes it's about doing what actually works for you.

—-

The Many Faces of Self-Care

1. Basic Self-Care: Showering, brushing your teeth, and drinking water (yes, these count).

2. Emotional Self-Care: Crying to Adele songs, journaling, or talking to your plants because they're the best listeners.

3. Practical Self-Care: Paying your bills on time or finally tackling that pile of laundry that's become a sentient being.

4. Fun Self-Care: Dancing like nobody's watching (because hopefully, they aren't).

—-

Part 2: When Self-Care Feels Impossible

Excuse #1: "I Don't Have Time"

Sure, you're busy, but you're also scrolling memes for 20 minutes before bed. Replace one meme session with something that makes you feel human, like stretching or reading a book. Or, if you're like me, stare at a wall in silence for five minutes—it's weirdly refreshing.

—-

Excuse #2: "I Don't Deserve It"

Yes, you do. I don't care if you accidentally sent a reply-all email to your entire office—you still deserve care. Your worth isn't tied to your productivity or how many salads you eat in a week.

—-

Excuse #3: "It's Too Expensive"

Self-care doesn't have to involve buying fancy candles or a gym membership. Affordable options include:

Screaming into a pillow (free).

Watching your favorite comfort show (also free, assuming you're still stealing your friend's Netflix).

Taking a nap (the ultimate budget-friendly activity).

—-

Part 3: Crafting Your Personalized Self-Care Plan

Step 1: Identify Your Needs

Ask yourself:

What makes me feel happy? (Answer: Probably not answering work emails at 10 p.m.)

What makes me feel relaxed? (Hint: It's not doomscrolling on Twitter.)

What recharges me? (Hopefully more than just caffeine.)

—-

Step 2: Add Self-Care to Your Schedule

Here's a revolutionary idea: Put self-care on your calendar. Treat it like an important meeting with yourself. And if someone tries to interrupt, just say, "Sorry, I have a very important appointment with Netflix and a weighted blanket."

—-

Step 3: Start Small

You don't have to overhaul your entire life in one day. Start with one small act of self-care, like drinking an extra glass of water or saying "no" to plans you don't actually want to attend.

—-

Part 4: The Self-Care Hall of Fame

1. The Nap

Taking a nap is like hitting the reset button on your brain. Bonus points if you manage to wake up and remember what year it is.

2. The Comfort Meal

Who cares if it's not "healthy"? If mac and cheese feeds your soul, then mac and cheese it is.

3. The Solo Dance Party

Put on your favorite song, close the curtains, and unleash your inner Beyoncé.

4. The "No" Practice

Learning to say "no" is peak self-care. Start small:

"No, I don't want to go to your cousin's cat's birthday party."

"No, I can't take on an extra project at work."

"No, I don't need a receipt for this gum."

—-

Part 5: Self-Care Fails (and Why They're Okay)

1. The Candle Catastrophe

You bought a candle for "relaxation" but accidentally set off the fire alarm. Self-care isn't always smooth.

2. The Yoga Disaster

You tried yoga and ended up falling on your face. Congrats—you just invented a new pose: "The Clumsy Warrior."

3. The Bath Bomb Betrayal

You finally tried a bath bomb, only to discover it dyed your skin pink. Lesson learned: Always read the label.

—-

Part 6: The Humor of Self-Care

Life is absurd, and so is self-care. Embrace the chaos. Laugh at the fails. Celebrate the small wins, like finally flossing for the first time in... let's not talk about it.

Self-care doesn't have to be serious. In fact, the more fun you make it, the more likely you'll stick to it.

—-

Homework: Create Your Self-Care Menu

Write down 10 self-care activities you can do anytime, anywhere. Here's an example:

1. Take a nap.

2. Watch a funny YouTube video.

3. Text a friend something ridiculous.

4. Take a walk and pretend you're the main character in a rom-com.

5. Eat dessert first.

Stick this list somewhere visible and use it whenever you feel overwhelmed.

—-

Final Thought: Self-Care is Self-Respect

At the end of the day, self-care isn't about being indulgent—it's about recognizing that you deserve kindness, even (especially) from yourself. So light that candle (carefully), take that nap, and own your self-care like the boss you are.

And next time you're in a freezing bubble bath, laugh it off. You're doing your best, and that's more than enough.

Chapter 4: How to Be Your Own Best Friend (Without Being Annoying)

The Mirror Pep Talk

There I was, staring into the bathroom mirror, trying to hype myself up for a big presentation. I leaned in dramatically and whispered, "You got this, champ."

And then I immediately burst out laughing because who says champ to themselves? But the weird thing is... it worked. That moment, ridiculous as it was, reminded me that if I don't have my back, who else will?

—-

The Concept of Self-Friendship

Think about your best friend. You'd hype them up before a job interview, celebrate their wins (big or small), and forgive them for eating your fries without asking. Now ask yourself:

Do you treat yourself with the same love and respect?

Odds are, you don't. Most of us are way better at being a friend to others than we are to ourselves. But here's the thing: You're the one person you're stuck with for life, so you might as well learn to enjoy your own company.

—-

Part 1: Why Being Your Own Best Friend Matters

1. You Set the Tone for How Others Treat You

If you're constantly tearing yourself down, it sends a signal to others: "Hey, it's cool to treat me like crap!" On the flip side, when you treat yourself with kindness and respect, people pick up on that energy and (usually) follow suit.

—-

2. You're Always There for You

Friends come and go. Relationships evolve. But you? You're there for every awkward high-five, every questionable haircut, and every late-night existential crisis. If you're not your own best friend, that's a long road to walk alone.

—-

3. Life's Too Short to Be Your Own Worst Critic

Imagine narrating your life as a sitcom instead of a tragedy. Your fumbles? Comic relief. Your triumphs? Standing ovations. Being your own best friend means seeing yourself as the lovable, flawed, and fascinating protagonist of your own story.

—-

Part 2: Signs You're Not Being a Good Friend to Yourself

1. You Talk to Yourself Like a Villain

Would you ever say, "You're such a failure," or "Why are you even trying?" to your best friend? No, because you're not a monster. So why do you say it to yourself?

—-

2. You Prioritize Everyone Else Over Yourself

If you're constantly saying yes to things you hate and no to things you need, you're treating yourself like an afterthought. A best friend wouldn't let you do that.

—-

3. You Never Celebrate Your Wins

When your friend nails a presentation, you're all, "YOU CRUSHED IT!" But when you succeed? You shrug it off like it's no big deal. Spoiler: It is a big deal.

—-

Part 3: How to Actually Be Your Own Best Friend

1. Master the Art of Positive Self-Talk

Instead of:

"I'm such an idiot for forgetting that!"

Try:

"Whoops, I made a mistake. It happens. Moving on!"

At first, this might feel awkward—like sending yourself a Valentine's card. But over time, you'll notice how much lighter life feels when you're not constantly roasting yourself.

—-

2. Schedule Quality Time With Yourself

Ever take yourself out on a solo date? No? Then it's time to start. Go to your favorite café, watch a movie you love, or even just take a walk and enjoy your own thoughts.

And no, this doesn't make you weird. It makes you someone who values their own company.

—-

3. Set Boundaries Like a Boss

Best friends have your back, which sometimes means saying "no" for your own good. Practice setting boundaries, even if it feels uncomfortable.

Example:

Friend: "Can you help me move this weekend?"

Old You: "Sure, even though I was planning to rest."

New You (best-friend mode): "Sorry, I can't this weekend. Let's catch up another time!"

Boundaries aren't mean—they're necessary.

—-

4. Celebrate Every Little Win

Did you make it through Monday without crying? Celebrate. Did you remember to water your plants? Throw a party (okay, maybe just a mini one). Being your own best friend means recognizing and appreciating your efforts, no matter how small.

—-

Part 4: The Hard Part – Forgiving Yourself

Why We're Harder on Ourselves Than Others

If your best friend forgot your birthday, you'd probably forgive them after some cake and a heartfelt apology. But when you mess up, you replay it in your head for days like it's a highlight reel of shame.

Here's a radical thought: What if you forgave yourself as easily as you forgive others?

—-

Exercise: Write a Forgiveness Letter to Yourself

Think about something you're holding onto—an embarrassing moment, a mistake, a regret. Now write yourself a letter like you're writing to a friend.

Example:

"Dear Me,

Okay, so you messed up. But guess what? You're human. Mistakes don't define you; how you learn from them does. I forgive you, and I hope you forgive yourself too."

Read it aloud if you can (yes, it feels weird, but it works).

—-

Part 5: Humor + Reflection = Growth

Laugh at Your Flaws

Being your own best friend doesn't mean pretending you're perfect. It means accepting your quirks and laughing at your missteps. Like the time you confidently used the wrong "your" in a heated debate. Oops.

—-

Ask Yourself Thought-Provoking Questions

1. If my best friend talked to me the way I talk to myself, how would I feel?

2. What would I do differently if I treated myself with the same kindness I show others?

3. What's one thing I could do today to make myself feel cared for?

Write these down and revisit them whenever you feel disconnected from yourself.

—-

Final Thought: The Power of Self-Companionship

At the end of the day, being your own best friend isn't about constant self-praise or ignoring your flaws. It's about showing up for yourself, even on the messy, awkward days. It's about being kind, honest, and endlessly forgiving.

Because the truth is, you're stuck with yourself for the long haul. So you might as well make the relationship a good one—filled with laughter, compassion, and maybe the occasional mirror pep talk.

Chapter 5: The Joy of Saying No (and Other Underrated Life Skil

The Great "Yes" Disaster

It all started innocently enough. My coworker asked, "Can you help me with this project?" Naturally, I said yes, because who doesn't love being a team player?

Then my cousin asked if I could babysit her three kids. Sure, why not?

Finally, a friend invited me to a weekend hike that started at 5 a.m. Did I want to go? Absolutely not. Did I say yes? Of course.

By Sunday night, I was lying on the floor, surrounded by spreadsheets, crumbs from my cousin's toddlers, and sore legs from the world's longest hike. My brain whispered, "Congratulations. You've officially ruined your life."

This was the moment I realized: Saying yes all the time is a terrible life strategy.

—-

Why We're Afraid to Say No

1. The People-Pleaser Problem

We've all been there: Someone asks for a favor, and before you can think, you blurt out "Sure!" Why? Because saying no feels like slapping them with a wet fish.

Spoiler: It's not. Saying no is setting boundaries, not committing social treason.

—-

2. FOMO (Fear of Missing Out)

Every time you say no to plans, your brain plays a highlight reel of everyone else having the time of their lives without you. Meanwhile, you're home in sweatpants, Googling "Can humans survive on cereal alone?"

Reality check: Most plans aren't as amazing as they sound. Plus, sweatpants and cereal are underrated joys.

—-

3. The Guilt Trip

Ever notice how some people have a PhD in guilt-tripping? They'll hit you with:

"But you're so good at this!"

"I thought we were friends!"

"This is the third time I've asked..."

Remember: Their guilt is not your responsibility. You're not a cruise ship captain trying to ensure everyone's smooth ride.

—-

Part 1: The Art of Saying No

Step 1: Reframe Your Mindset

Saying no doesn't mean you're lazy, selfish, or mean. It means you're prioritizing your energy and sanity. Imagine your time and energy as a pie chart. Do you really want to give 90% of your pie to things that exhaust you? Save a slice for yourself.

—-

Step 2: Master the Polite Decline

Here are some go-to phrases:

"I wish I could, but I'm already swamped."

"Thanks for thinking of me, but I'll have to pass."

"No, but I hope it goes well!"

For those persistent guilt-trippers:

"I understand this is important to you, but I can't commit right now."

"No. And that's my final answer. (Cue dramatic music.)"

—-

Step 3: Practice in Low-Stakes Situations

Start small. Say no to that free sample at the grocery store. Say no to the barista asking if you want whipped cream (okay, maybe not that one). Build your "no" muscle so it's strong when you really need it.

—-

Part 2: The Benefits of Saying No

1. More Time for What Matters

Every "no" is a "yes" to something else—like sleeping in, binge-watching your favorite show, or finally trying that hobby you've been putting off.

2. Less Stress

When you stop overcommitting, you also stop feeling like you're constantly sprinting on a hamster wheel. Spoiler: Hamster wheels aren't a good look on anyone.

3. Stronger Relationships

When you set boundaries, the right people will respect them. The wrong ones? Well, let's just say they might need some time to re-evaluate their entitlement.

—-

Part 3: How to Spot a "No" Situation

1. The Gut Check

When someone asks you to do something, pause and ask yourself:

Does this bring me joy? (Marie Kondo would be proud.)

Do I actually have time for this?

Am I only saying yes because I feel guilty?

If the answer is "no" to the first two or "yes" to the last one, it's time to say no.

—-

2. The "Will This Matter in 5 Years?" Test

Your friend's cousin's wedding on a Wednesday afternoon in another state? Probably not. Spending quality time with your family or recharging your batteries? Absolutely.

—-

3. The "Do I Want to Punch Myself Later?" Rule

If you're already dreading the thing you just agreed to, future you is going to be pissed. Save yourself the internal yelling match and say no upfront.

—-

Part 4: The Humor of No

1. The Overdramatic No

Sometimes, you've got to make it fun:

"Oh no, I'd rather wrestle an alligator than do that."

"Sorry, I'm allergic to events that start before noon."

—-

2. The Disappearing Act

When you can't say no, sometimes you just... vanish. (Not recommended for serious commitments, but for group texts planning a karaoke night? Totally fair game.)

—-

3. The "Blame Your Pet" Excuse

"I can't; my cat gets separation anxiety."

"Sorry, my dog's birthday is that day."

(Yes, you can make up a pet if necessary. Who's going to check?)

—-

Part 5: Life Skills You Unlock When You Embrace "No"

1. The Power of Prioritization

Saying no forces you to think about what truly matters to you. Spoiler: It's not your coworker's improv class showcase.

—-

2. The Gift of Alone Time

When you stop overcommitting, you suddenly discover the joy of doing absolutely nothing. Imagine: no plans, no stress, just you and your favorite blanket. Bliss.

—-

3. The Ability to Spot Manipulation

Once you get good at saying no, you'll notice how often people try to guilt, bribe, or sweet-talk you into things. It's like unlocking a superpower.

—-

Homework: Your "No" Cheat Sheet

Write down five things you're going to say no to this week. For example:

1. That work meeting that could've been an email.

2. The PTA bake sale (store-bought cookies count).

3. Driving someone to the airport at 4 a.m.

4. A weekend party when you'd rather Netflix and chill (alone).

5. Joining that pyramid scheme disguised as a "business opportunity."

Stick to your guns, and don't feel bad about it.

—-

Final Thought: Saying No is Saying Yes to Yourself

Every time you say no, you're reclaiming a little piece of your life. You're giving yourself permission to rest, recharge, and focus on what truly matters. And honestly? That's one of the most badass things you can do.

So go ahead, practice your "no." Say it with confidence, humor, or even a touch of sass. Because life's too short to spend it doing things that drain your soul.

Chapter 6: The Magic of Letting Go (Without Setting Everything on Fire)

My Closet of Emotional Baggage

It started with a single shoebox. "I'll just keep this as a memory," I told myself, placing it in the corner of my closet. Fast forward five years, and my closet looked like a time capsule of regret. Old birthday cards from people I hadn't spoken to in years, clothes I hadn't worn since the Obama administration, and, for some reason, a VHS tape even though I haven't owned a VCR since middle school.

One day, while trying to shove another "sentimental" item into the chaos, the closet door burst open, and everything spilled out. My cat stared at the mess, silently judging me. It was time. Time to let go—not just of the junk in my closet but of the emotional baggage I'd been hoarding alongside it.

—-

Why Letting Go is So Hard

1. Nostalgia's Sneaky Grip

We convince ourselves that every item, every memory, every ex deserves a shrine. "But this mug reminds me of that time I had coffee with Janet from accounting!" Cool story, but Janet left the company four years ago, and the mug is chipped. Let it go.

—-

2. The Fear of "What If"

What if I need this someday? (Spoiler: You won't.)

What if I forget this memory without the physical reminder? (You won't. And if you do, maybe it's not worth remembering.)

Letting go feels like closing a door, but sometimes that door leads to a room full of spiders. It's okay to close it.

—-

3. Emotional Hoarding

We don't just hoard objects—we hoard grudges, failures, and bad decisions like they're collector's items. "Oh, this guilt from that time I said the wrong thing in 2012? Better keep that forever."

Spoiler: Emotional baggage doesn't increase in value over time. Toss it.

—-

Part 1: The Benefits of Letting Go

1. You Make Space for New Stuff (Literally and Figuratively)

When you clear out the clutter—whether it's physical junk or emotional weight—you create room for new opportunities, new experiences, and, let's be real, new throw pillows.

—-

2. You Stop Carrying Dead Weight

Imagine hiking up a mountain while dragging a suitcase full of regrets. Sounds exhausting, right? That's what holding onto old baggage feels like. Letting go is like finally ditching that suitcase and sprinting to the top. (Or, you know, leisurely strolling because cardio is overrated.)

—-

3. You Learn to Laugh at the Past

Once you let go, you can look back and chuckle. "Remember when I cried for three days over that breakup with Kyle? What was I thinking?" (Spoiler: You weren't. But it's okay.)

—-

Part 2: How to Let Go Without a Breakdown

Step 1: Sort Your Stuff (Physically and Emotionally)

Think of it like a garage sale for your soul. Go through everything and ask:

Does this serve me anymore?

Does it make me happy, or does it make me cringe?

Am I keeping this because I genuinely want it or because I feel obligated?

If the answer is "cringe" or "obligation," toss it.

—-

Step 2: Forgive, but Don't Forget to Be Funny

Forgiveness doesn't mean you have to send your nemesis a fruit basket. It's about releasing the grip they have on your mental real estate. Example:

"I forgive Chad for stealing my lunch that one time. I hope he enjoyed my sandwich. It was dry anyway."

Humor makes forgiveness easier—and slightly petty, which is a win-win.

—-

Step 3: Do a Letting-Go Ritual (Yes, Seriously)

Write down everything you want to let go of on a piece of paper.

Dramatically rip it up, burn it (safely), or flush it down the toilet like it's a bad script idea.

Bonus points if you play a dramatic soundtrack while doing it. (May I suggest "Let It Go" from Frozen?)

—-

Step 4: Replace the Old with Something New

Every time you let go of something, replace it with something that actually brings you joy. Toss those toxic friends? Make room for people who hype you up like a personal cheer squad.

—-

Part 3: The Hilarious Things We Hold Onto

1. Ancient Text Conversations

Why do we keep screenshots of arguments with exes? Are we planning to present them in court someday? Unless you're starring in a Netflix true-crime series, delete them.

—-

2. Clothes That Don't Fit

Ah yes, the jeans from high school. We keep them as if they're some magical talisman that will shrink us back to our teenage size. Spoiler: They're not. Donate them and buy jeans that fit your fabulous self now.

—-

3. That One Friend Who Drains Your Soul

You know the one. Every text feels like a homework assignment. "Ugh, what now?" If their presence stresses you out more than it lifts you up, it's time to gently (or not-so-gently) let them go.

—-

Part 4: Humor in Letting Go

1. The Roast Your Baggage Method

"Remember that phase where I was obsessed with succulents and killed every single one? RIP, Planty."

"Wow, I really thought bangs were a good idea in 2019. Bold of me."

Laughing at your past makes it easier to move on.

—-

2. Turn it Into a Game

For every item you let go of, reward yourself:

Toss old clothes? Treat yourself to ice cream.

Delete toxic contacts? Buy yourself that ridiculous mug you've been eyeing.

Gamifying the process makes it less painful and way more fun.

—-

Homework: Your Letting-Go Challenge

1. Write down three physical items, three memories, and three emotional weights you're ready to let go of.

2. Commit to letting go of at least one from each category this week.

3. Celebrate with something ridiculously indulgent (like a bubble bath or a nap that lasts way too long).

—-

Final Thought: Let Go Like a Boss

Letting go isn't about pretending the past didn't happen. It's about giving yourself permission to move forward without dragging all the junk behind you.

So go ahead, release the old, embrace the new, and maybe even set some stuff on fire (safely). Because life's too short to hoard regrets, grudges, and VHS tapes.

Unpacking the Emotional Suitcase (Literally and Figuratively)

Why Are We Like This?

We have a weird attachment to stuff. Remember that sweater your ex gave you? The one that's three sizes too big and smells like regret? You don't wear it, but somehow it's still hanging in your closet like a ghost of bad decisions.

Then there's the pile of birthday cards. Sure, Aunt Carol's message was sweet, but is "Have a great year, love Carol" really worth prime real estate in your drawer? Spoiler: No.

—-

Step-by-Step Guide to Saying Goodbye

1. The Brutal Honesty Test:

Hold each item and ask: "Do I love this, or am I just scared of throwing it away?"

If you hesitate for more than three seconds, it goes. Yes, even the shirt from that 5K you walked three years ago.

2. Personify Your Junk:

Pretend the stuff can talk.

The VHS tape: "I don't even know why I'm here!"

The chipped coffee mug: "Please, let me rest in peace."

Sometimes, a little humor makes it easier to part ways.

3. Divide and Conquer:

Make three piles:

Keep: For the genuinely useful or joyful stuff.

Donate: For the things that can bring someone else joy.

Trash: For the things that should've been thrown out during the Bush administration.

Unpacking the Emotional Suitcase (Literally and Figuratively)

Why Are We Like This?

We have a weird attachment to stuff. Remember that sweater your ex gave you? The one that's three sizes too big and smells like regret? You don't wear it, but somehow it's still hanging in your closet like a ghost of bad decisions.

Then there's the pile of birthday cards. Sure, Aunt Carol's message was sweet, but is "Have a great year, love Carol" really worth prime real estate in your drawer? Spoiler: No.

—-

Step-by-Step Guide to Saying Goodbye

1. The Brutal Honesty Test:

Hold each item and ask: "Do I love this, or am I just scared of throwing it away?"

If you hesitate for more than three seconds, it goes. Yes, even the shirt from that 5K you walked three years ago.

2. Personify Your Junk:

Pretend the stuff can talk.

The VHS tape: "I don't even know why I'm here!"

The chipped coffee mug: "Please, let me rest in peace."

Sometimes, a little humor makes it easier to part ways.

3. Divide and Conquer:

Make three piles:

Keep: For the genuinely useful or joyful stuff.

Donate: For the things that can bring someone else joy.

Trash: For the things that should've been thrown out during the Bush administration.

—-

How to Let Go of Emotional Clutter

Physical clutter is just the appetizer. Emotional baggage is the main course.

The Ex Files

Why are you still stalking your ex's Instagram at midnight? Unfollow them. Block them if necessary. Their brunch photos aren't that interesting, and you deserve peace.

—-

The "Should've" Collection

"I should've gotten that promotion."

"I should've apologized to my friend sooner."

"I should've been nicer to the barista who spelled my name wrong."

Newsflash: The past is not a Netflix series you can rewind. Let it go, or it'll keep renting space in your brain for free.

—-

The Grudge Bucket

Holding a grudge is like drinking expired milk—you're the only one suffering. Imagine your grudge is a balloon. Now picture yourself letting it float away. Or, better yet, pop it with a satisfying "pop!"

—-

The Magic of Moving On (with Style)

Forgiveness is Freedom: Picture forgiveness as handing back a backpack full of bricks. "Here, this is yours. I'm done carrying it."

Decluttering is Empowering: The less you carry, the more you can focus on what truly matters—like finding room for that air fryer you've been eyeing.

—-

Closing Thought:

Letting go isn't about losing something; it's about gaining space for new, better things. Whether it's an open closet or a lighter heart, you're making room for a brighter, funnier, and freer future.

Chapter 8: Repacking the Suitcase of Self-Love

Chapter 8: Repacking the Suitcase of Self-Love

After spending Chapter 7 emptying out my emotional baggage (and probably finding some things that should have stayed packed, like that one pair of socks that just don't go with anything), I realized something important: It wasn't enough to just throw the old junk out. I needed to replace it with things that made me feel light, empowered, and ready to take on the world – or at least, tackle my day without looking like I'd just rolled out of a tornado.

This is where the art of repacking comes in. And let me tell you, it's not just about putting the "good stuff" in. It's about strategically choosing what belongs in your life – and what absolutely does not. Trust me, you don't need to carry around the emotional equivalent of a ten-ton suitcase for the rest of your life.

Step 1: Acknowledge the New Items You're Adding

Self-love isn't just about eliminating negativity; it's about actively adding things that nurture you. This might sound easier said than done, but think of it like shopping for groceries: You know you need to buy healthy foods, but you're so tempted by that bag of chips. (Which, by the way, we all know you'll regret by the time you reach aisle three.)

Here's the kicker: With self-love, the healthy "groceries" are things like boundaries, gratitude, self-compassion, and permission to rest. So go ahead, fill up that emotional suitcase with these high-vibe essentials, and throw out that self-doubt snack pack that has been sitting in there way too long.

Step 2: Embrace the Luggage Organizer

Ever tried to fit everything you own into one carry-on bag? It's a disaster. So why do we expect our emotional suitcase to be any different? The key is organization – and by that, I mean understanding the difference between your emotional essentials and the stuff you think you need but really don't.

You may have noticed I didn't mention the "guilt" section. That's because guilt is an emotional item we often hold onto without realizing we don't need it. It's like that one T-shirt you haven't worn in five years but still can't bring yourself to get rid of. If you have guilt weighing you down, it's time to donate that baggage. You're allowed to live without it.

Step 3: Pack Your Own Energy (and Not Just Your Friends' Expectations)

One of the biggest lessons I learned on this self-love journey is that I had to reclaim my energy. For years, I packed my suitcase with everyone else's needs, wants, and expectations. But if I'm being real here, it felt less like "self-love" and more like a human-sized packing crate that was just about to explode.

Self-love doesn't mean being selfish, but it does mean being self-aware. This means understanding that your time, energy, and emotions are valuable resources. So instead of trying to meet everyone's demands (and then wondering why you have a breakdown on Tuesday), you pack in your own needs first.

Which brings us to Step 4...

Step 4: Leave Room for Fun and Spontaneity

You've packed your emotional suitcase with the essentials. Now, here's where the fun part comes in: Leave some space for the unexpected. Life isn't all about structured routines and organized chaos. If you pack too tightly, there's no room for joy, laughter, or the occasional adventure.

So, once you've got your boundaries, your rest, and your self-compassion all tucked away nicely, remember: Leave a little room for the stuff that makes you smile. Maybe it's an impromptu dance party in your living room or a solo trip to the ice cream shop. Whatever it is, make sure your suitcase has room for play.

Step 5: Check the Zipper

Finally, once your emotional suitcase is packed, it's time to check the zipper. Is it secure? Are you able to carry it confidently, without worrying it might burst open at the seams? If yes, then you've done the work – and it's time to head out on your self-love journey.

If not, don't panic. There's always room for more reflection and adjustments. Life is a journey, and sometimes your suitcase might need a little rearranging. Just make sure you're not carrying things that no longer serve you.

Chapter 9: Self-Love Isn't a One-Time Thing (It's More Like Relearning to Dance)

I had this brilliant idea that self-love was a one-time transformation. I thought I could just figure it out, click my heels three times, and BAM – I'd be this enlightened, calm, centered person, floating around like I was in an Instagram ad for yoga. You know, all white clothes, sipping herbal tea, never having a hair out of place.

But that's not how this works. No, self-love is a lot more like trying to learn the cha-cha while your two left feet are stuck in cement. It's awkward, you might trip, and sometimes it feels like you're just waiting for the music to start playing again. But here's the thing: Even when you mess up, you're still moving forward. And if you trip and fall? It's still part of the dance.

Step 1: Realizing That Self-Love Isn't a Magic Trick

I used to think self-love was something that happened all at once. Like a lightbulb moment – a sudden realization that I was worthy and great and everything would now be sunshine and rainbows. One day, I thought I had it all figured out. I took a deep breath, looked at myself in the mirror, and said, "I am enough." Then I tried to float across the room, imagining a montage of inspirational music playing in the background.

Unfortunately, what followed was less of an empowered glow and more of a mild panic attack when I realized I still had an inbox full of emails that made me feel like I was drowning. And that's when it hit me – self-love isn't a quick fix. It's more like training for a marathon than crossing a finish line.

Self-love is not a magic trick. There's no wand that makes you a perfect human. There's no fairy godmother that grants you immunity to awkward situations and self-doubt. Self-love is something you practice every day – even when it's inconvenient, even when you'd rather hide under a pile of blankets and pretend the world doesn't exist for a few hours.

When I got upset about something, I used to instantly go into "fix-it mode" – trying to solve the problem before I even had time to process my emotions. But now? I've learned to just sit with the discomfort. That's the magic of self-love: it's learning to be with yourself, even when you're not feeling like your best self. Because those moments are just as valid as the ones when you feel like you've got everything figured out.

Step 2: Embracing the Inner Critic (And Telling It to Take a Seat)

If there's one thing I've learned about self-love, it's this: There's always that voice. You know the one. The inner critic. It's the voice that sneaks up on you, just when you start feeling good about something. Like, "Wow, I've made so much progress!" and then bam, that voice chimes in, "Sure, you've made progress, but you're still not perfect. You haven't achieved your goals yet. You didn't do enough today."

At first, I thought the only way to practice self-love was to eliminate that voice. I figured if I could silence my inner critic, then I'd truly love myself. But here's the thing: That inner critic is always going to be there. It's like the guest at your party who refuses to leave, even when everyone else is having a good time. No matter how much self-love you practice, it'll always pop up, especially when you're about to do something that scares you.

So what do you do? Do you kick the inner critic out? No. You simply tell it to take a seat and relax. It doesn't get to control the show. For me, when the voice pops up, I've learned to acknowledge it without giving it the spotlight. Like when you're at a party and someone starts talking about a topic that you know is going to be a disaster, you don't have to engage. Just nod politely, and move on.

Self-love is recognizing that you're worthy even when the inner critic shows up. You don't have to wait for that voice to go away to love yourself. It's like dancing with an awkward partner. You can still sway, even if they keep stepping on your feet.

Step 3: Dancing Through the Awkwardness

Let's talk about the awkward moments of self-love. Because they are a lot more common than you think. The first time I tried to consciously practice self-love in public, I was at a coffee shop, feeling like a whole new person – confident, radiating positivity, glowing from the inside out.

I walked up to the counter, smiled at the barista (who I'm sure thought I was a little strange), and ordered the most indulgent latte on the menu. Extra foam, because I deserve it.

I walked out of the shop, holding my latte like it was a trophy, thinking, "Yes! I am practicing self-love right now. I am a glowing goddess, worthy of all the foam!" And then I saw my reflection in the coffee shop window.

Now, you might think I was about to be hit with a wave of self-love perfection. But instead, I saw myself: slightly disheveled hair, a little too much mascara, a slightly crooked smile, and oh wait – was that a spot of latte on my shirt?

For about three seconds, I felt like I had completely failed. Like maybe self-love wasn't meant for me because clearly, I didn't look like the confident Instagram version of myself. But then I remembered: self-love is about accepting yourself, even in those moments when you feel a little ridiculous.

And you know what? I smiled. I didn't care about the latte stain or my hair. I had the foam, and that was enough.

That's the beauty of self-love. It's not about being perfect. It's about embracing your imperfections and laughing at them. Because if you can laugh at yourself, you're already ahead of the game.

Step 4: Self-Love on the Bad Days

Let's get real for a second. Self-love isn't just about the good days. It's about the bad ones too. There are days when I wake up, look at myself in the mirror, and think, "What is happening? Why am I still wearing pajamas at 2 PM? Why do I feel like I've been hit by a truck?"

On those days, self-love isn't about doing a full-on face mask or journaling for an hour about how amazing I am (although, those things help). It's about giving myself permission to have a bad day. On my worst days, I've learned to say, "It's okay. You don't have to be perfect. You don't have to get everything done today. You just have to get through it. And that's enough."

Sometimes, self-love means just curling up in your comfiest hoodie, watching your favorite show, and eating takeout while pretending to be a professional couch potato. And honestly? That's perfectly valid.

Because self-love isn't about achieving perfection or always being on your A-game. It's about being kind to yourself when you're not at your best, and recognizing that you still deserve love, even on the days you're not exactly feeling it.

Step 5: Reaffirming the Dance, Even When You Fall

By this point in my journey, I've learned that self-love isn't about arriving at some final destination where everything is perfect. It's more like a dance, a series of steps that you keep practicing. Sometimes you'll glide gracefully, other times you'll trip over your own feet. But the important thing is that you keep going. You don't stop dancing just because you miss a beat.

And honestly, it's the awkward moments that teach you the most. Because when you fall, you get up. When you stumble, you laugh. And when you're feeling down, you remind yourself that this is all part of the process.

Self-love isn't a straight line. It's a winding path full of zigzags, unexpected turns, and sometimes, a misstep here and there. But that's what makes it beautiful – it's messy, imperfect, and real. And it's your dance.

Chapter 10: The Final Step – Self-Love Doesn't Mean You Have to Ignore the Signs

Here we are. Chapter 10. The grand finale. The last step on this wild, awkward, and occasionally messy journey of self-love. You've unpacked your emotional suitcase, learned to wade through your inner critic, laughed at your own awkward moments, and realized that self-love is more like a dance than a perfect performance. And now, we're here to wrap it all up in a bow.

But before we do that, let's get one thing straight: self-love isn't about ignoring the signs—whether that's in relationships, your own emotions, or your physical well-being. If anything, self-love is about paying attention to those signs. In fact, self-love is all about knowing when to stop dancing, take a break, and recalibrate. It's about understanding your worth—not just on your good days, but on your bad ones too.

So, let's talk about that. The truth is, self-love is not about becoming a walking, talking Pinterest board of happiness and positivity. You can't just plaster motivational quotes over everything and expect your life to magically be without bumps. Self-love is about recognizing your value and listening to yourself—your body, your mind, your soul—when it's trying to tell you something.

You know those moments when you feel like the universe is practically throwing a tantrum trying to get your attention? The signs are flashing neon, but you keep ignoring them, hoping that if you just push through, everything will work out. That's not self-love. That's self-denial wrapped in a snazzy self-help book cover. And, trust me, the universe will not be fooled.

Step 1: Don't Be the Human Ostrich (Put Your Head Out of the Sand)

There's this tendency we all have to ignore the signs when things aren't right. I used to be an expert at this. When I was in a toxic relationship or working in a job that made me want to throw my laptop out the window, I'd tell myself, "Just push through! It'll get better. Maybe tomorrow. Probably tomorrow. Definitely tomorrow."

But here's the thing about ignoring the signs: It doesn't make them go away. In fact, it usually just makes them louder. If I've learned anything in this journey of self-love, it's that your body, mind, and heart will scream at you when you're out of alignment with your true self. The trick is to listen before the screaming turns into full-on chaos.

Let's be real: we all know when something feels off. Whether it's a job you dread, a relationship that's draining you, or a project that leaves you feeling like you're running on fumes, there's a voice inside you that's giving you the memo. You might try to drown it out with noise or distractions, but that little voice will keep coming back. Self-love isn't about ignoring that voice; it's about acknowledging it and making adjustments.

Step 2: Self-Love Means Knowing When to Say "Nope, Not Today"

As much as I love a good motivational quote, I've realized that self-love is not about saying "yes" to everything in the name of being positive. It's about knowing when to say "nope, not today." And trust me, this is the most liberating skill I've learned in my adult life.

We've all been there, right? You're asked to take on another project, attend a gathering that sounds like a low-key nightmare, or lend a friend your favorite hoodie (which, let's face it, is probably never coming back). And then comes the internal tug-of-war: "But I should say yes. It's a good opportunity. I don't want to let anyone down."

Let me just say it: self-love is about saying no without guilt. It's about knowing your limits, respecting your boundaries, and not feeling like you have to apologize for it. You don't have to be available to everyone all the time. You don't have to overextend yourself in the name of being liked.

Self-love is recognizing that your time and energy are precious, and if something doesn't align with your values, it's okay to say "no thanks."

Now, I know it's easier said than done. There's a little voice that pops up, trying to convince you that you're being selfish or rude. But the truth is, saying "no" isn't a negative act; it's a self-preserving one. It's a way to honor your emotional and physical well-being. And hey, if you really want to take it a step further, you can always follow up with a solid excuse like, "Sorry, I've got a prior engagement with my couch and Netflix."

Step 3: Knowing Your Worth Means Not Settling for Less Than You Deserve

Here's the thing about self-love: once you start practicing it, you realize that you're worthy of so much more than you've been settling for. I spent years in relationships, jobs, and situations where I was constantly giving and never receiving the respect or appreciation I deserved. But once I started valuing myself, I realized I was worth more than those situations.

Now, self-love isn't about being perfect or thinking that you'll somehow be exempt from challenges. It's about recognizing that you deserve to be treated with kindness, respect, and love, and you don't have to accept anything less.

For me, this came with a big realization in one of my past relationships. I had been sticking it out, convinced that if I tried hard enough, I could fix things. But self-love hit me like a ton of bricks: it wasn't about fixing something broken—it was about realizing that I didn't need to fix myself to deserve love. I was worthy of love just as I was, flaws and all. And once I truly accepted that, it became clear: I didn't have to settle for less than I deserved.

This realization didn't come overnight, and it definitely wasn't easy. But once I embraced it, everything shifted. I started surrounding myself with people who respected me, set boundaries that honored my needs, and stopped tolerating things that made me feel less than amazing.

Self-love means knowing that you deserve the best, and not being afraid to walk away from anything that doesn't align with that.

Step 4: It's Not About Perfection—It's About Acceptance

One of the most important lessons I've learned on this journey is that self-love isn't about perfection. In fact, it's the exact opposite. It's about embracing your imperfections, your mistakes, and the parts of yourself that you'd like to change—not as flaws, but as beautiful parts of who you are.

We are all flawed. We all have those awkward, messy, imperfect moments. But that's what makes us real. Self-love isn't about striving for some unattainable version of yourself where everything is always going according to plan. It's about loving yourself, even when you're messy.

Here's my final piece of advice: Don't wait until you're perfect to love yourself. Love yourself in the midst of the chaos. Love yourself when you've eaten an entire pizza by yourself (it happens). Love yourself when you're feeling down, when you're not at your best, and when you've just had the worst day ever. Because those are the moments that matter. That's when self-love counts the most.

Step 5: The Grand Finale—You Are Enough

So here we are, at the end. You've made it through all the awkward steps, the bumps, and the hilarious missteps of this journey called self-love. And I want to leave you with this simple truth: You are enough.

It's not about being perfect. It's not about having it all together. It's about understanding your worth, loving yourself even when you fall, and never settling for less than you deserve.

Now go ahead. Keep dancing. Keep stumbling. Keep laughing at yourself, because you are doing better than you think. And above all else, never forget your worth. The journey doesn't end here. In fact, it's just getting started.

Epilogue

The Journey Continues

As I sit here, reflecting on the words of this book, I can't help but smile. There's no perfect ending to this journey—no moment where everything suddenly falls into place and you become a glowing beacon of self-love. Instead, there's an ongoing process, a continual dance with yourself, where some days you glide, and some days you trip. And you know what? Both are okay.

This book isn't about handing you a one-size-fits-all solution. It's about sharing the messy, beautiful, sometimes awkward path I've walked in the hopes that you'll find a little comfort and humor in your own journey. The truth is, we're all still learning. Even after all the breakthroughs, the realizations, and the "aha" moments, there are still days when I wonder if I'm doing it right. But here's what I've learned: there's no wrong way to practice self-love. There's only the way that works for you.

What I hope you take away from these pages is that self-love is an evolving journey. It's something you can return to again and again, with compassion for yourself and for where you are today. It's about understanding that you are always enough, even when you feel like you're "still figuring things out" (because, spoiler alert, we all are).

This isn't the end of the story. It's just a chapter, and it's up to you to keep writing your own. It's up to you to continue learning how to embrace your imperfections, laugh at the messiness, and keep loving yourself—no matter what.

So, as you close this book, take a deep breath. Celebrate how far you've come and the work you've put into your own self-love journey. But also remember: this isn't a destination. It's an ongoing practice. There will be times when you forget your worth. There will be days when you stumble. But there will also be moments of triumph, moments of clarity, and moments where you realize just how much you've grown.

And when those tough days come—and they will come, because life is both beautiful and challenging—remember that you are worthy of love. You don't have to be perfect to be loved. You don't have to be flawless to be enough. You are, in this very moment, exactly who you need to be.

So go ahead. Keep learning. Keep laughing. Keep growing. The dance of self-love isn't about perfection; it's about being kind to yourself, no matter how you look or feel in the moment. You are worthy. You are enough. And above all, you are deserving of all the love you can give yourself.

And if nothing else, never forget: it's okay to dance awkwardly.

Don't miss out!

Visit the website below and you can sign up to receive emails whenever S. Page publishes a new book. There's no charge and no obligation.

https://books2read.com/r/B-A-KMPZC-XSDMF

BOOKS 2 READ

Connecting independent readers to independent writers.

About the Author

S. Page is a multifaceted creative professional, An accomplished Author, Filmmaker, Actress, Director, Editor, Writer and Producer. Hobbies: Loves to write in free time, anime, martial arts, traveling, speaking, k-dramas, comedy.

www.ingramcontent.com/pod-product-compliance
Lightning Source LLC
LaVergne TN
LVHW090128160826
845673LV00015B/1102

* 9 7 9 8 2 3 0 5 7 3 9 0 6 *